Life Recovery for the Cluttered Soul

how to face your fears and transform your life

Artwork: Leigha Diesel

Patricia Diesel

Keep It Simple Now, LLC

Life Recovery for the Cluttered Soul
Copyright © 2015, Patricia A. Diesel

Keep It Simple Now, LLC
14 Cottage Street
Basking Ridge, NJ 07920

www.keepitsimplenow.com

All rights reserved. No portion of this book may be reproduced in any form or by any electronic or mechanical means including information storage and retrieval systems without express permission of the author. The scanning, uploading and distribution of this book via the Internet or via any other means without the permission of the publisher is illegal and punishable by law. Please purchase only authorized electronic editions and do not participate in or encourage electronic piracy of copyrightable materials. Your support of the author's rights is appreciated.

ISBN: 978-0-9789303-2-5
Library of Congress # - 2015904228

All information in this book is the result of the author's experience, research, or common sense. The intent is to offer information of a general nature to support you in your emotional and spiritual well-being and physical clutter. This is not a prescribed form of treatment for any physical, emotional, or medical problems. In the event you use any of the information in this book for yourself, the author and the publisher assume no responsibility for your actions.

Quotes from copyrighted sources are listed and credited accordingly. Any mention of brand name, company, or website should not be considered an endorsement, as the author has no affiliation with brand name, company, or website, and is not paid to endorse any product.

This book is dedicated to my Parents...
Thank you for loving me.

"There's no book that tells you so
Only love can guide you through
Judgment calls in the night
Praying you will get it right
As only Parents come to know
Fearful nights and tearful fights
Broken hearts that leave you blue
Scolding here yet tender there
Never too far out of sight
One day when it's said and done
And spirits fly and souls reunite
I'll find you easy and all so well
As only Children come to know."

~PGD

Contents

Foreword vii
Dear Friend xiii
Introduction xix
Family Influences 1
  My Mother's Purse 7
Cluttered Souls 15
  George 18
  Karyn 23
  Dan 28
  Timothy 33
  Jonathon 38
  Leonia 43
  Sean 48
Path to Recovery 55
  Facing Our Clutter Fears 56
  Life Coaching & Professional Organizing 62
Personal Assessment Guide 67
About the Author 79

Foreword

In the Beginning...

"I absolutely DO NOT NEED an Organizer!!!!" That was me in March 2014 as I growled at my friend Jane, who was diligently, but unsuccessfully, trying to motivate me from California. Jane had read about Patricia Diesel and "Keep It Simple Now" on the Internet and thought that an organizer might be the answer to getting me "unstuck."

"Stuck" was the understatement of the century. I was in a logjam, and I needed a lumberjack with a sack full of dynamite to get me moving again. Inertia. Distraction. Procrastination. Dread. All these words meant nothing to me in my earlier life where I had worked as a business analyst, project manager, bank vice president and independent consultant. They also meant nothing to me as a wife, mother, homeowner, world traveler, and volunteer. However, I had suddenly just stopped in my tracks, unable to move forward with my life or able to make major decisions affecting my future. I was nearing a crisis point in my life, and I was totally unable to function. I needed something…someone…to unblock me, and I needed it immediately, whether I liked it or not!

So, I called Patricia and nothing will ever be the same.

The Process

"I absolutely DO NOT NEED an Organizer!!!!" I said as I spoke to Patricia on the phone. She did not buy my reluctance. However, she listened patiently as I ticked off my delusions of competency, independence, and functionality. When I finished explaining why I did not need her, she

gently asked, "How is that working for you? And how can I help?" Well, this was different! She saw right through my defensiveness, but she was not finding fault, psychoanalyzing me, or giving me Gestapo orders! She kept it simple, and asked how she could help. This was a kind, human offer. I was in it for the long haul. I WOULD GET ORGANIZED in spite of myself!

We met at my pleasant but cluttered townhouse in New Jersey. She asked me not to put anything away or straighten up, which was surprisingly difficult. What would she think? As she assessed my situation, I gave her some of my background, and we made a pact to speak for an hour once a week to create a manageable plan of small steps to achieve big results. Patricia came one day with an associate, and the three of us completely decluttered my dining room, living room, and kitchen in less than three hours! For months, I had only been able to move a few things from one pile to another and made no progress at all. The secret, as Patricia showed me, was to make decisions to keep, donate, or dispose of items while someone else was helping me. This way it was easier to keep emotions out of the decision-making process, and not re-bond with the memories attached to those items. How simple!

The Emotional Component

My rainclouds began late in 1998 with the death of my mother, which was followed six weeks later by the death of my brother. Two more deaths, my father and my husband, occurred shortly after. I sold my home in Freeport, New York, and moved to a lovely townhouse in New Brunswick, New Jersey, to be closer to my son. I had a walled garden, a stream, and all the nature I ever wanted. It was peaceful and serene.

I healed and made myself happy and useful as a family support leader at

Habitat for Humanity. More rain was in store, as I lost another brother and helped a close friend pass her final days at my home. I was devastated and depressed by those losses and began my slide into clutter from that time. My physical health deteriorated, as well as my emotional health, and I needed a pacemaker and constant monitoring.

My son, who had moved back to New York when he got married, was furious with me for staying in New Jersey, as I was facing such high risks to my health. He wanted me closer so that he could be there for me, but I interpreted that as trying to run my life. I needed to sell my townhouse, relocate, find local doctors, and rebuild the relationship with my son. These needs were all major tasks, and before I began to work with Patricia, I was incapable of starting, or even prioritizing, any of them.

The result, with my eternal thanks to

Patricia Diesel, is that I staged and sold my townhouse, moved back to New York, and now surround myself with the love of my son and daughter-in-law, my family, and my life-long friends. I am managing my health, and I am happy to be back among people I love. My house is organized (I will give myself a B-), and when I say that I am a "work in progress," I mean it. I really mean it.

~*Barbara Elsherbini*

Dear Friend

Long ago, I made a promise that this book would come from a place of raw honesty, with the hope that whoever may be reading it will not feel alone. Therefore, I would like you to know that I truly do understand the depth of one's pain and sorrow. If in some small way these words bring you comfort and a better understanding of "things," then I feel honored to have contributed to that.

After several defeats in my personal life, I was searching for something that would bring me a sense of comfort, stability, and a deeper understanding of myself. But what? Everything felt so out of reach. This was the point where I knew I needed to do something to get my life back on track. As scary as it was at times, I started to take a serious and intimate look into my life. The revelations I found opened the door to my own life recovery.

You see, there was a time in my life when my world appeared to be going great…and then everything changed. Personal challenges of health, finances, and my relationships became too difficult to handle and got the best of me. It was as if everything that I believed in came crashing down. I felt completely broken.

I remember the pain I felt. I also remember that all I wanted was for the pain to go away. I wanted to give up. But instead, I allowed myself to feel the pain. I cannot really explain it, but I ended up relinquishing myself to a place of surrender. I just had no other choice but to experience it.

Afterwards, when all was quiet and still, I began to feel a sense of peace.

This peace provided me with the courage I needed in order to have a very spiritual conversation with myself. This inner dialogue brought about clarity, along with the hope that things will get better. Of course, I cannot minimize the fear I felt during this process. Recognizing the need for change can be difficult enough; acting on it is a huge step, and one I do not take lightly for myself or for others.

It took some time, but little by little, I could feel myself changing. I started reading everything I could get my hands on that helped me make sense out of what just happened. I started to attend workshops and seminars. I followed and listened to people from whom I could learn. I became inspired!

My inspiration turned into an idea. That idea turned into a vision. I took that vision and created action steps. Those actions changed everything and birthed my professional organizing and life coaching business. More importantly, it taught me invaluable lessons about the power of our undying spirit and human will.

I am forever grateful for my experience, as it has brought me to a place of appreciating the value of true love, unconditional acceptance, reverent forgiveness, and pure gratitude. For without being broken, I would not have witnessed the bearing of my soul and the loving hand of God.

Please understand, I am not suggesting that it takes one to be broken in order to have a relationship with God. (Or however you may choose to refer to your Creator or a Higher Power.) What I am expressing is my acknowledgment and testimony to my own experience that has provided me with the gift of understanding myself.

A portion of this book is devoted to the stories of people who had their own journey of recovery to navigate. It is my desire that their inspiration will further encourage others to look inward and see that we can all take the necessary steps towards inner peace and happiness.

I believe sharing is a part of caring. Therefore, I hope whoever reads this will discover just how much I really do care.

In Healing,

Patricia Diesel

Introduction

"Nothing clutters the soul more than remorse, resentment, and recrimination."

Norman Cousins – Author of *Head First* and *Anatomy of an Illness.*

If you picked up this book, it is probably because you, or someone you care about, have decided that changes need to occur in order to lead a better life. Coming to that realization is a big step for everyone, but the next phase is equally difficult. **"What are the changes I need to make and how do I go about doing it?"**

This is the first question anyone has to ask before we can begin the process of Life Recovery. Life Recovery is about thriving again. Life's difficulties build emotional blocks up in all of us. Sometimes they are temporary obstacles and, at other times, they become full-fledged walls. It is my intention that this book will guide you over, around, and through those blocks to a better place in life.

There are a countless number of events that can impact a life and knock even the strongest individual into a sense of desperation and hopelessness. Some examples are:

- Divorce
- Ending of a relationship
- Care giving
- Illness
- Death
- Career changes
- Financial distress

It has been my experience that these events can create an inner conflict. This struggle can result in the outward manifestation of physical clutter and emotional blocks, as the stories in this book will reveal.

We are all human, and there will be times when we will hurt. That is when we realize just how fragile we are. Because we are delicate, a person may not cope with a life-changing event very well. The frustrating part is when a person recognizes that they are captured by an unforgiving cycle of behaviors and do not know how to get out of the situation.

The premise for writing this book is due to the simple belief that nobody should have to overcome life's difficulties alone. When you feel lost and have no one to talk to, it can be heart wrenching. I understand the pain and suffering that someone goes through, and I realize that support is paramount to the healing process. Inspiration and encouragement are key ingredients for one to regain hope and move forward with life.

This is why I have provided stories

of people, just like you and I, who have faced adversity in their lives. Understanding what they went through may help you gain further insight and clarity with *your* challenges. With my chosen profession comes an obligation to be the "secret keeper." These stories are very real; however, I have modified the circumstances and characters to protect the identity and privacy of those involved. I present these real life experiences as a sampling of human challenges and the perseverance we have in each of us to overcome them.

Likewise, I am not a psychologist or any other type of mental health professional. Indeed, as a certified professional coach, I ask my clients if they are under the care of a physician for any maladies. Sometimes circumstances may suggest such care. The fact is that my work enables me to share the joys and hurts of their lives, and this has sharpened my perception of human nature. That insight is what I offer to others, and it has helped me present these stories to you. My hope is that my experiences can be a beneficial tool in your life.

Family Influences

I have seen that relationships can profoundly affect our lives. I know they have with me. We begin at an early age to feel the influences of the family unit, which can vary for each of us. Families come in all different blends and styles, and thus create our earliest experiences — both positive and negative.

It is important to take note that we all have events in our lives that create our own unique experiences. These experiences have emotional attachments based on our thought processes — which in turn create our reality.

To paraphrase Neale Donald Walsch: Events do not create our reality; it is the experience of the event that does so. The emotion that we attach to the event is what creates the experience. What creates the emotion to the event is the thought. Why are thoughts different amongst people? It's because it's the truth we have about the event. (I highly recommend you read Neale's library of books – beginning with "Conversations with God" – for additional insight into this.)

As you will see from these stories in this book, this makes perfect sense when we look at how we carry "things" around from our past and how this can affect our present life. These things may manifest into physical clutter and/or emotional blocks due to the truths we have been telling ourselves.

This simple teaching has helped me immensely with my family experiences. At this point in my life, I feel extremely fortunate and grateful for my childhood. However, I did not always feel that way. I had a very slanted perspective on the way I was raised, especially when it came to my mother.

One could say that in some regard I had a very strict upbringing, which in the same vein forced me to become self-sufficient — or as I saw it then — to fend for myself. I did not like, much less understand, why at such an early age I had to adopt such stringent domestic duties. Instead of playing house, like most kids, I was living it on a daily basis. This created an extreme amount of pressure for me, and I constantly worried if I was doing everything right.

Although I was not able to comprehend it at the time, I felt there was something missing between us. I would watch my friends interact with their moms and noticed how different our relationship was. My mom was caring in a lot of ways, and was very generous with providing me emotional outlets, such as dance classes and other social activities, but communicating her love was not her strength. With the innocence of a child, I craved to feel her love in a way that can only be shared in the physical intimacy of an embrace. I just wanted her to hug me. I wanted to feel protected. And most of all, I wanted to hear the words "I Love You."

For years, I struggled with abandonment issues. It would surface in friendships, relationships, my marriage, and yes, even in my very own parenting. The thought of someone leaving me kept me in a cycle of fear. A fear so deeply rooted that it felt impossible to ever change it, much less me understanding it.

They were not my finer moments, for sure, and I have regret over many things I have done; but today, I have a deeper insight into it all. I have come to learn that regret is actually a good thing. Regret is a sign of personal growth from which we can learn, if we detach this word from shame and guilt. Most people associate regret with remorse, and therefore are caught up in this terrible cycle of feeling bad about themselves. Regret shows us that we are different now, and we would no longer choose to do things that may be hurtful to others or ourselves.

Please allow me to share with you a very personal and intimate story of my childhood years. I refer to this time as *childhood bruises*. I tell you this because I want to give you hope. Hope that one day you too will have clarity and peace of mind. It is my intent that it will give you additional wisdom into how I used the tool of compassion to help embrace a fuller and richer understanding of another's pain (my mother's) to bring about freedom, and yes, love. I call it **My Mother's Purse**.

My Mother's Purse

I am looking at it now, my mother's purse. It is a small leather change purse with tarnished brass handles. You know the kind where the handles twist together in order to click them open. The leather, a deep royal blue, still has its luster after all these years.

It never fails; with just one "click," I return to being a child. I am eight years old and searching for my mother's change purse. The change purse is inside her pocketbook, which she always leaves on the living room stairs.

I am still not sure how this ritual came to be, but every morning before I go to school, I go on a treasure hunt in search of lunch money that I can only find in my mother's change purse. I kneel down on the steps, and as I rummage through her pocketbook, I feel frantic yet confused at the same time. This morning routine makes me feel unsure about everything at this point in my young life.

I only have a certain amount of time left. I just finished making my breakfast, getting myself dressed, and now I have to walk to my girlfriend's house a couple of blocks away to catch my ride to school. What I do not understand is why I have to do this by myself.

There is a heaviness in my chest as I hold back my tears. I feel scared because I know that once I do find the money, I will leave for school without saying good-bye to my mom. I feel uneasy, because I am not sure why she is not with me. I feel a separation, a detachment…a longing for my mom to be with me, but she never comes.

It hurts — the pain that this childhood memory causes. Why doesn't it ever go away? You would think by now that it would not bother me so much, but year after year, it is still with me.

But today...

With just one "click" of my mom's purse, it brings me back to a place of seeing my mom for who she really was. Whatever my mom was going through in those years, I am sure it was difficult for her. I can now see that she managed the very best way that she knew how to at the time. Despite what I went through, it did not mean she did not love me.

In hindsight, I choose to believe that she did her very best with the model of the world she had. This helped me to stop blaming her for my own unhappiness and to accept the fact that she really did love me. It may not have been the way I would choose to be loved or to love, but it did not negate the fact that she did love me.

Thinking of her love, I remember throughout the years her unwavering faith in me. Whenever I would go to my mom and share my concerns and fears with her, her reply would always be the same. "Patty" she would say with a smile, "you will be all right. You will manage and land on your feet. You always do, you know."

The words she said were so comforting to me. It is funny; even if I did not believe it, I found solace in the fact that she did. It was as if she always knew something that I did not. This was especially true on the days when I felt that I was not going to be okay.

Today, when I reflect on my mom's words, I say to myself, "Yes, Mom, you were right. I have landed on my feet." In fact, as I look back on my childhood with a clearer eye, I can see how this experience has prepared me for my life's work. It forced me to be extremely organized. For example, these are some of the things I learned to do as a young girl:

- Clean
- Vacuum
- Dust
- Laundry
- Iron
- Make my bed
- Prepare meals
- Cook
- Wash/dry dishes
- Select wardrobe

These household tasks may seem like ordinary domestic chores, but for a young person it taught me how to manage my time, have a keen eye for detail, develop a sharper perception, and nurture an overall innate knack for sorting *things* out. I also came to realize that this was a "gift" I could share with others.

Whenever I look back on the emotional pain I navigated growing up, I am in awe of the "gift" of compassion it has taught me, and I marvel at the fulfilling life it has provided. And I fall to my knees each and every time I realize this truth and say, "Thank you, God. Thank you!"

Cluttered Souls

As you read this collection of stories, one aspect I hope you see in them is how our life is inseparable from our souls. C.S. Lewis once said, "You do not have a soul. You **are** a soul. You have a body."

Have you ever met someone that you just connect with — you know, where everything just feels easy and simple? Connecting with that person is like the feeling of a hand in a glove or an old pair of slippers. This is how I like my relationships with my clients to develop: with that soul-to-soul connection.

I believe that our souls resonate deeply with one another, and that we get glimpses of who we truly are — therefore the saying, "the eyes are a window into one's soul," makes perfect sense to me. I choose to believe that before we were born, we made a conscious choice as souls to collaborate collectively through our life's journey. It is my calling to help on that journey.

I also believe that a great life means bringing peace to our souls. Relinquishing painful experiences and learning how to "let go" helps the soul be free. When our mind, our body, and our environment are cluttered, our soul's light becomes dull and cries out to shine and be healthy. A cluttered soul invites and manifests illness, which can come in many forms of disease and disorders. If we took a moment to examine the accumulation of clutter from this perspective, I think we might gain valuable insight.

It is such an undeniably remarkable gift — our souls. They are deserving of nourishment and light. My desire is that one day all our souls will shine brightly. This is my prayer.

ALL I SEE IS YOU

In my strangest dreams
Through nights of feverish screams
I don't know what it means
But all I see is you
And when I've run too far
Chasing that lonesome star
I don't know who you are
But all I see is you...

~Author Unknown

George

Long before I truly understood what path I was heading towards, I accepted my very first invitation into the world of recovery. This was the recovery from clutter in someone's life.

By now, people were starting to know a little bit about me, and the services of a professional organizer. I am still to this day not clear on how I got the reputation of "the keeper of one's secrets," but that is one way that people knew me. You see, behind one's clutter are usually shame and guilt, so having the assurance of confidentiality provides peace of mind to be able to open up and share.

One morning, I received a phone call from a gentleman, and the first thing he asked me was my policy on confidentiality. I assured him that it was a cornerstone of my professionalism. He liked that, so I encouraged him to tell me more about why he was calling me. He introduced himself as George and explained that his office was bursting at the seams with paper, and that he was in desperate need of organization.

George greeted me at his beautiful office building with a great big smile. We made small talk for a bit in his lovely reception area, and then I asked him if he was ready to show me his office. He let out a deep sigh with a small chuckle, as he nodded in agreement. As he escorted me down the hallway, he tried to mask his anxiety with idle chatter and humor.

As we approached the office, George became silent. He turned to me and quietly whispered, "I can't believe I am going to show you this." I reassured him that it was time, and it would be all right. He took a deep breath, closed his eyes, and pushed the tall, carved oak doors open.

Stepping in, all I could see was that every surface was completely covered by piles of paper stacked higher than you would think possible. The floor was one big layer of paper that resembled little peaks and valleys, and although I knew there was furniture in the room, it was barely visible.

I stood in wonderment of it all. It was as if it rained paper.

I realized that this was going to take a courageous and ambitious effort on both our parts. It was a huge endeavor. It would require me to give him my full attention and successfully guide him to sort through everything. George was making a commitment to finally go to the places inside himself that he had been avoiding. I had no idea at the time how taxing this would be on both of us.

George and I worked together for just over five months. As we navigated our way through his piles — purging and sorting — we were also uncovering some very important events that took place in George's life. I found out that his mom had passed on, and George was very close to her. He looked to her not only as a mother, but also as a mentor and a friend. They were in the same profession and had professionally collaborated on projects. We found an unfinished business plan that they were working on together before she died. The concept was to franchise their business, and the document was only half done. They never had a chance to finish it.

At the time of his mom's death, there were some other relationship challenges in George's life, primarily in his marriage. It was clear that he was suffering and doing his best to "keep up appearances." This is why he confined his clutter to his office. No one else could see his secret here. George's paper clutter was an outward manifestation of his inner pain. The emotional distress from the loss of his mother was evident in the way he chose to accumulate papers. The unfinished business plan was an obvious example illustrating how George was dealing with his loss. There was no reason that George could not have continued working on the franchise proposal on his own. Deep inside, though, he believed that acting on the papers in his office was somehow putting distance between himself and his mother. Emotionally, he needed guidance to help him through this.

As George worked through the papers, he simultaneously worked through his grief. He came to understand that releasing the papers was about letting go and saying good-bye to his mom. He also realized that there were other options available for him to honor and keep his mom's memory alive.

Karyn

At first sight, Karyn appeared confident and compelling. Speaking with her, I detected a high level of intelligence, the innocence of a young girl, and the charming curiosity of a child. Yet, like a slow-moving current that has a strong tow, I sensed something was brewing deep inside that she was trying to contain.

Karyn's primary complaint was that she was having difficulty maintaining her home, while trying to balance her new life as a single mom and the demanding pace of her career. She confided in me that this was creating a problem for her children. She was fearful that this was a reflection of poor parenting skills, and it would get back to her ex-husband.

From assessing the conditions of her apartment, it was clear that Karyn was not struggling so much with organization as she was with her domestic duties. When they were married, Karyn had the better job and was the primary breadwinner. Maintaining the house was not something she had to be concerned about. Now, however, she faced these additional responsibilities and was completely overwhelmed.

This was evident by the piles of pots and pans, weeklong dirty dishes and utensils, empty bags and containers of food that were all over the kitchen counters and appliances. The bathroom had not been cleaned in months and was not suitable for necessities, much less to shower and bathe in. Magazines and newspapers were scattered about the floor.

The children's bedroom showed signs of linens in need of laundering, food debris, and a random collection of toys. Shoes and clothes were thrown about haphazardly. The surface of their dressers were covered with hair accessories, figurines, and excess clutter. The remainder of the home, which consisted of the family room, office, and Karyn's bedroom, were relatively neat and tidy. I found this to be interesting.

It was obvious to me that beneath these unkempt areas of the home lay dormant resentment and distress due to the separation of her marriage. Karyn was not only angry, but she also felt conflicted about the new role she was playing in her domestic life.

I suggested to Karyn that she was not necessarily so much in need of a professional organizer, but rather, in desperate need of a cleaning service. Karyn shared with me some challenges she faced growing up with her mother, which directly influenced her marital relationship and the way she viewed domestic roles.

Karyn's aversion to cleaning was centered around unresolved feelings from her childhood that were triggered by the anger she was feeling towards her ex-husband. Her built-up resentment manifested in a rebellion against authority figures, being told what to do, etc. This ultimately manifested in her clutter and unwillingness to clean.

While my recommendation of a cleaning service solved the immediate practical problem, there was a lot more work Karyn needed to do in order to get a handle on some deep-seated emotional issues. You can see how her early family life directly affected her current family, as Karyn came to realize through our work together.

The beauty and the gift about the process of getting one's self organized is that it can reveal certain behaviors and patterns. This can provide the opportunity to further explore why he or she may be doing things a certain way. Most often the answers are enlightening, which can help us face our fears, bring us to a deeper understanding, and transform our lives.

Dan

When Dan contacted me, he was very soft-spoken, and I could detect sadness in his voice. He said that he had read an article of mine on Life Recovery and could identify with what I had to say. Because he saw bits and pieces of himself throughout the article, it peaked his curiosity and gave him the courage to call.

I asked Dan what he thought was his biggest struggle, and he confessed that it had to do with his challenge of keeping up with his paperwork. I asked him if he experienced this challenge at both work and home. Dan responded that at work he did not feel he had any problem with organization and efficiency, so that confused him as to why he was unable to deal with this in his personal life.

Upon further questioning, he shared with me that most of the paperwork had to do with the settlement of his grandmother's estate. He explained to me that since she had passed away, he was unable to open any of his mail. Yet, he was able to manage his household bills, which only made him feel even more confused.

Dan was aware enough to know that he was experiencing an emotional reaction to the paperwork, but was not able to identify its source. All he knew was that every time he would attempt the paperwork, he would experience extreme anxiety — to the point where his arms would tingle, his heart would race, and he would feel pain in his chest. This cycle was then compounded by the sleepless nights spent worrying and beating himself up.

His grandmother had raised him, and she had been rather well off. Her portfolio included an abundance of investments that either needed to be cashed in or converted over. There were stacks of uncashed checks that may have reached their expiration date. There was also legal and tax paperwork that needed immediate attention. This all became very overwhelming for Dan.

I suggested to Dan that I guide him through the process of opening the mail, sorting it out, and then organizing it as a first step to help him overcome his angst. He agreed. I then advised him on what organizing tools to purchase in order to prepare for our organizing session. I told him we would need some time together to conquer the first stage of his project.

The two of us were able to open, sort, purge, and organize his grandmother's paperwork that pertained to all areas of her estate. Through this process, Dan was able to clearly see what was in front of him without it feeling too overwhelming or intimating.

It turns out Dan and his grandmother did not have such a great relationship while he was growing up. He confessed to me that his grandmother was a very controlling woman, and his memories of her were not very fond ones. Since Dan did inherit the total estate, including the home he now resided in, it only fed into his existing feelings of guilt and shame.

Dan always felt ridiculed and that he never lived up to his grandmother's standards, so his emotional block was due to his inability to believe that he could conquer the "financial" aspect of her estate without somehow screwing it all up. I encouraged him to see how courageous he was to reach out for support and to take on this project.

I explained to him that going through the process of working through the paperwork, he was actually reclaiming his power. At the same time, he was recovering and healing from his *childhood bruises* and transitioning into a self-sufficient adult who made wise and healthy financial choices.

Timothy

Sometimes even the happiest, most successful person can be brought to his or her knees by a life-changing event that shatters their foundation.

Such is the case of Timothy, a young, handsome father of three.

When Timothy first contacted me, he shared with me that it was difficult for him to get out of bed in the morning. After he got his kids off to school, all he wanted to do was go back to bed and sleep the day away. Timothy's wife had recently died. Self-employed and working from home, he was struggling financially. He left a good job to work from home and take care of his kids. On top of the normal bills, he was also accumulating college tuition debt while pursuing another degree. Timothy was literally worried sick over how he was going to manage it all.

Exploring Timothy's situation a little deeper, it became apparent that he was feeling anxious due to his lack of mobility. He was not used to staying "still" even for the slightest moment. Any time Timothy had "nothing" to do, it would create a deep sense of fear that he was not working hard enough, which only fed into his deeper core worries that his dreams of making a better life for himself and the children would not come true. To quiet himself down in troubled times such as these, Timothy would turn to addictive behaviors that led him to self-loathing and depression. This was why he could not muster up the strength to get out of bed.

As Timothy and I worked together, I suggested that we begin to look at other possibilities to produce income. He invested so much of his time in dwelling on his "lack" that he exhausted himself emotionally and mentally. I wanted him to see that by refocusing his attention away from the problem and looking at the situation as an opportunity, we could find viable solutions for him. This was also a tool to help him tap into his dormant gift of creativity.

I also encouraged Timothy to consider implementing mantras as part of his daily regiment to restore his wellness and attraction to wealth. One in particular that I fell in love with, and have committed to memory, is by Bob Proctor: "I am so happy and grateful now that money comes to me in increasing quantities, through multiple sources on a continual basis." I have found this simple mantra to be very powerful.

Slowly but surely, Timothy began to get excited. The idea of being his own boss gave him hope, as it indicated the possibility of creating a better life. It also gave him a sense of control over his life that helped remove the cycle of feeling victimized.

It is important to note that as we worked together, Timothy began to see that he was not alone in his situation, and that there were plenty of men who faced similar challenges in life. As he came to identify with this truth, Timothy began to put on his thinking cap. He confessed that he had long desired to start a landscaping service and thought this might just be the ticket to get his life back on track.

Step by step, we began to conceptualize a business plan. With lots of love and hard labor, Timothy gave birth to his new business and this energetic, feisty, young man was back at work, *literally*!

Through this experience, Timothy was able to get in touch with the part of himself that he feared the most and tried so desperately to run away from:

The fear that he could not manage his home, kids, and business on his own.

The concept of starting a business tapped into his entrepreneurial spirit and gave him wings to fly. It represented hope that he would not have to ever feel that his life was at any time in the hands of someone else. He realized that he did have the ability to make choices for himself — choices that would enhance his life and the welfare of his children.

Jonathon

It can be terribly sad when a person is getting ready to say good-bye to this life. However, the experience of working with such a person preparing for their farewell is, well, almost indescribable. It is beyond a privilege and an honor. It is a gift.

When you are invited into someone's life at this time, you quickly recognize that you are participating in the grandest celebration of their life, as they put the final touches on their legacy. This very deep and meaningful bond always touches my soul.

To say Jonathon touched my soul is an understatement. Interestingly enough, Jonathon put up an on-line request for a professional organizer to help him get his house in order. It was during the cold of the winter, and since he lived in a warmer climate, I was up for a little sunshine and some adventure. I decided to contact him.

I found Jonathon to be whimsical. A talented writer who could compose fiction or fact-based articles on anything, he had such a light-heartedness in his view of life. Although Jonathon was well into his late seventies, he was young at heart, with a romantic flare in just about everything he spoke about. His spirit knew no boundaries, and I simply found him intoxicating.

The initial request was to get the house in order while decluttering his life. That is all I knew at the time. But once Jonathon and I began our work together, it was apparent that there was much more to this story.

The main thrust of our work was to "let go" of the things that he was ready to part with, as he came to accept that his children would not want these things if he left them behind. With that in mind, our efforts began. Some of these things were books, clothes, paper, and just "stuff" that one acquires over the years. I did not find anything necessarily different or unordinary abut his request.

That is until it came to his children's things. This is where the floodgates opened.

You see, Jonathon knew his time was limited here with us, although he never spoke of it or brought it to my attention. Once we started going through his children's things, I began to understand what was really going on. Jonathon's overall mission was to somehow memorialize his fatherhood. He wanted to figure out how to capture the highlights of his children's events while they were growing up. He was obviously a special father and wanted to express those years of love and devotion he treasured.

The surprise was, unbeknownst to me, one of Jonathon's children was a famous athlete. This made the experience even more fascinating. Sorting through all of the belongings and keepsakes was truly a treasure and a walk down memory lane for both of us. We shared a special mission together, as we attempted to put together Jonathon's legacy.

Now mind you, it was not always easy. There were times of difficulty. Heartstrings were tugged and resistance was present, but eventually the job got done. We devised treasure boxes to honor the special occasions that would capture the stories Jonathon was trying to convey for his special message to his children.

The remains of the house never were addressed...at least not with me. Although Jonathon's initial request was for help with getting his "things" in order, it became apparent that establishing a legacy for his children was truly the agenda. Once this was completed, my time and purpose was fulfilled.

Jonathon rewarded me in kind with two VIP tickets to see a game his son was playing in New York City. It was such a special treat and paid perfect tribute to Jonathon's legacy.

Leonia

"Are you the Clutter Lady?" the voice asked on the other end of the phone.

"Why yes, I suppose I am," I said with a slight chuckle.

"Good, then I'm in the right place," she said with a slight sternness to her voice. I quickly detected that this woman clearly wanted to get down to business.

It was not long before I received the most concise, snappy version of Leonia's life. Although her overall tone was sharp, there was a particular tenderness about her that I found endearing.

I quickly learned that Leonia was now retired and living an entirely different life than she envisioned for herself. In the prime of her life, Leonia held a prominent position at a major magazine. At that time, she was the minority in a predominately male environment. Leonia recognized early on that she had to work and play hard in order to earn her keep. Talent alone was not going to keep her there.

Leonia made her career the primary focus of her life and climbed the corporate ladder to financial success. She was able to buy fancy cars, vacations, and homes, but she was never able to buy herself the one thing that she desperately longed for — love.

She reflected back for a moment to a time when finding love appeared hopeful. There was a boy that she dated in college, but unfortunately, he did not live up to the expectations of her parents. They instilled in Leonia that she could do better and that she should set her sights on a different type of love. In time, Leonia went on to find that different type of love. For her it was her work, while her college sweetheart went on to marry.

I know this because when I questioned Leonia about her clutter, she became very remorseful and insisted that if she would have married, her life would never have turned out this way — full of chaos.

Upon my visit to Leonia's, it was evident that she needed immediate care and support. Her environment was in disarray on so many levels, with trash and clutter throughout all the rooms of her home.

What stood out for me was the love affair she had with her clothes. Leonia's wardrobe was the only part of her clutter that she regarded with care. Even though there were clearly piles of clothes scattered about her home, and nothing was in their proper place, Leonia could still point out and tell me what was in every pile and where everything was.

The fascinating thing here is that although she had no regard for the other things in her home, she made it a point to have her clothes stay a priority and had them professionally laundered on a weekly basis.

I feel this was Leonia's way of staying connected with the identity of her younger years, when things appeared to be happier and there were remnants of love. It was also a way for her to keep herself hanging on to life the best way she knew how. As long as she had her clothes, she could remain hopeful that not all was lost.

Leonia also shared with me that her financial investments were depleted during the height of the financial collapse. It appears, according to her, that she fell prey to a financial heist and was swindled out of her fortune.

To compound an already emotionally wrought situation, Leonia moved back to the apartment where her parents had raised her. It was rent controlled, and this aspect continued, which helped Leonia's financial situation. On the other hand, it also added some additional insight into Leonia's family. She shared with me some of the family history that indicated the possibility of emotional and mental health challenges. In some ways, the apartment may have not have been the healthiest environment for Leonia.

I did the best I could to help her. However, as time went on, I could see that she needed different help than I was able to provide. In the best interests of Leonia, I managed to get in touch with a distant family member to help facilitate the best medical and emotional care for her. I am grateful that she did get in touch with me, and I was able to offer help and guidance.

Sean

One cannot imagine the depths of a parent's sorrow when losing a child. Unless you have walked this path, it is difficult to know how you would cope, much less manifest your pain.

This was the case with Sean.

When Sean contacted me for the first time, he told me that he and his wife attended one of my speaking engagements years back on Chronic Disorganization. We spoke on the phone for a while, and he expressed his worries and concerns about clutter. He shared that when his wife was alive, they had clutter, but it only grew worse after she passed away. He felt that he was finally ready to resolve his disorganization and wanted to set up an appointment with me.

We scheduled his consultation and assessment. However, a few days later he called and cancelled.

During the next couple of years, Sean and I would exchange emails or periodic phone calls, but he still could not bring himself to make another appointment. Finally, Sean contacted me one day and told me his life had changed dramatically, and time was no longer on his side. He had terminal cancer. He told me the idea of leaving this life without having his "things" in order was too much to bear. He was now ready.

Sean's home is best described as a hodgepodge of excess clothes, books, paper, and unfinished projects. It was not hard to figure out his patterns based on the trail of laundry, unwashed dishes, and piles of unopened mail. Clearly, Sean was struggling for a very long time.

Due to the nature of his condition, he

expressed to me that his full purpose behind decluttering was to somehow make things "right" again. There were things that just felt really out of sorts, although he could not put his finger on one specific thing. There was a deep desire to scale down, sort it all out, and put it back together again.

I suggested that our work should begin in the garage first. I explained my thinking to him and said we would need to have an area that had clear access so that we could bring things in and out of the house. It would also be a place for displaying items that he wanted to give away. He agreed.

At the time, I was not sure why I felt so strongly about starting with the garage. Initially, I thought it was just the organizer in me who was planning efficiently. However, today I see it quite differently.

You see, Sean's garage was filled with so much more than just the ordinary tools and gadgets one finds in a cluttered garage. By working in Sean's garage, I discovered why Sean could not manage to ask me to come to his house for years. Sean had a secret…a very big secret.

The answer to Sean's shame and guilt lay deep within all the clutter and debris. Underneath it all was a part of his past that he tried to put to rest. This was the only way he knew how to keep his deep, deep sorrow from surfacing.

Buried under everything was a box of a child's belongings. This child died young, and Sean and his wife had put every photo and item of their child in a large carton and placed it in the garage. That was sad enough to me, but what shook me to my core was when I asked Sean about a sealed container in the box; he told me it was the urn containing the child's ashes. Over the years, accumulated stuff slowly buried the box. It was as if the child's memory was buried amongst the chaos of life. Sean had continued to try to desperately block it all from his memory, yet never managed to close it off from his heart. Why Sean and his wife chose the garage is still a mystery to me, but I am sure it can be interpreted in many ways.

It would be amiss of me to not share my *initial* reaction of shock and distressing sadness. The profoundness of that experience drained my spirit and left me overwhelmed for days. I could not fathom how one could possibly be that disconnected to their own extension of life.

But you see, *I had it all wrong.*

Neale Donald Walsch once said to me, "Patricia, there will come a day when you will see the beauty and gift and the pure perfection of such a tragedy, where you will fall onto your knees and say 'Thank you, God. Thank you.'"

My clients expose themselves to me. They are vulnerable and emotionally naked, revealing their innermost secrets and feelings. At times, they are so brutally raw that I wonder how they manage to survive.

Today, I see the gift I received through Sean and some of these other clients I mention, and all of the untold stories. I understand that I witnessed the essence of human frailty. It has changed me. It has changed me in a way that has created a new layer of compassion. I have a much deeper level of unconditional acceptance for people and what they go through in life. And for that I do say, "Thank you, God. Thank you!"

Path to Recovery

Facing Our Clutter Fears

As you can see by the stories I told, when it comes to clutter, there can be many reasons why someone is fearful. They may be afraid that if they let something go, they may need it again, or they will not be able to replace it.

You see, many times clutter represents chaos and being out of control. For others, it can also be a source of comfort. Comfort in a way where *things* replace or serve as a substitute for an area of one's life that may be in distress.

It is understandable that one may "think" this, especially when the reason they hold onto their stuff for so long is that it helped them through some difficult times. Hence, "letting go" may trigger other emotions that can create a sense of loss, etc.

Fear is part of being human, and there can be many layers of fear. Underneath these layers is usually something we are terribly afraid of.

So how do we fight fear? By facing it head on.

Here is where knowledge about one's self becomes your best strategy to fight your fear. Why? It is impossible to control something that you know nothing about. However, you can control your outcome from what you understand. Therefore, understanding what is driving your fear helps you not only confront what you are afraid of, but also helps you fight back and change it.

Let's take a hypothetical situation and use this as a case in point. Let's say you have a house full of clutter. Your desire is to be organized and orderly. However, you have much fear when it comes to releasing your stuff. Yet, you feel equally fearful that if you do not do something about it, it will really get out of control.

One approach to overcoming your fear is to create a vision of what you would like to see happen for yourself. An example would be, "I would like to have more open space in my home and have everything in its place." Then take a moment to visualize what that may actually look like in your home.

Next, ask yourself, "Why is this vision important to me?" A simple answer may be, "I am tired of not being able to find my things and spending too much time looking for them."

Another question from there may be, "How would this vision affect the quality of my life?" An answer may be, "It would make my life more manageable, reduce stress, and give me peace of mind."

Now, let's look at this together. You have a house full of clutter. You want to be clutter free, because you understand that it will provide you with a better quality of life. This much we know so far. Yes?

Okay, now we get to the good part: Facing the fear head on!

So let me ask you something. "If you want all these things that you say you do, what's stopping you?" You may answer with something like this, "Well, I've tried many times before, but I never succeeded. And I guess in truth, I am afraid that I may need my things one day. So if I get rid of them, I won't be able to get them back."

Aha! There it is. The thought that you planted in your head that you will never be able to recover something is so ingrained that it paralyzes you from moving forward with your vision.

And the truth is that the chances of you never really being able to find, obtain, or purchase those "things" again is pretty slim. This is an untruth you told yourself that you "bought" into. For this reason, it makes you feel terribly afraid. (It's important to note that something of significant value or uniqueness would not fall into this category.)

This is a story of fear, but underneath all those layers is an untruth. In part, it has been the story you may have been telling yourself all this time, because in some way it was helping you cope with something that may have been causing you distress. Therefore, "letting go" may symbolize for you a loss of not having something important in your life when times get tough. *"For, if not for your clutter, what would you cling to?"*

It is fascinating, isn't it?

The good news is that today, you

know better. By facing what you are truly afraid of, you have the power to change it. You know this is just an old story that keeps replaying, over and over. All you have to ask yourself now is, "How would your life be different if you were able to overcome this?"

Just imagine the possibilities for you!

Life Coaching & Professional Organizing

Although my chosen profession of life coaching has many facets to it, as you have seen by the stories in this book, a central role that I take on is one of being a professional organizer."

Many people I work with have a high degree of clutter in their life. As a professional organizer, I assist them in a supportive, nonjudgmental manner within a tailored, highly personalized approach to recovery. Having an organized framework to establish order to personal and professional affairs helps restore sanity and peace to one's life.

At times, the client requires additional hand-holding, so making suggestions, providing advice, and giving one-on-one assistance is necessary to help facilitate the process of recovery. In order to better understand and address a client's needs and wants, a seasoned professional organizer will ask the right questions. This requires a keen set of listening skills. Organizers must be compassionate, responsible, professional, and have the ability to physically and mentally guide the process for the client. This involves breaking down goals into manageable steps by visualizing the bigger picture, and putting a plan together to meet objectives.

As you can see from these stories, the circumstances that affect each one of us are as different as our individual fingerprints. This is not a situation of "one size fits all." For some, it is getting a handle on a life that was turned upside down from sickness, divorce, death, or any number of difficulties that can hit us. Others may simply wish to enhance where they are in life and do not know how to go about it. As I have learned, each person I work with on his or her road to Life Recovery requires flexibility as well as attention to detail. These are keys to overall success.

The professional life coach is an individual who will work closely with you to help you maximize your life in any area you know you need help: career, relationships, personal growth, etc. Whether you need help in one area of your life or a combination of them, a professional life coach works with you to create a strategic plan to achieve your goals.

From an organizational standpoint, I like to think of this as having your very own "toolbox." This is a unique one-on-one partnership built on trust without judgment. You have your very own personal mentor that provides knowledge, insight, and support.

The backing of a trusted mentor is a huge factor in achieving personal goals. While the process may become emotional, professional life coaching is different from traditional therapy in that it does not dwell on psychological issues. It is a proactive, progressive life changer designed to meet your physical, emotional, and/or spiritual needs.

Remember, the stories I have related here are only the tip of the iceberg. I have personally dealt with many more in my chosen calling. The unfortunate problem is that for every instance I have helped someone, there are hundreds of other stories out there. The stories are of people who are hurting and who do not know where to turn for help. You may be one of them, or know someone who needs help.

As you have seen, Life Recovery does work. By dealing with the issues and clutter that have gotten into the way of life, you are giving yourself a gift — the peace of your soul. This is something that none of us should deny ourselves.

Personal Assessment Guide

- Print out this Assessment Guide before you start this book so you can write down your notes or any insights as you read.

- Think of the key areas of your life from which you feel you need to recover. How would your life be different if you worked on these?

- As you read, write down any "aha" moments that you may experience — these are important insights, so you do not want to lose them.

- Consider how you can begin implementing any changes that resonate the most for you throughout this book.

From what area of your life do you feel you need to recover?

How long have you been struggling with these challenges?

Do you believe in God or a Higher Power?

_____
_____
_____
_____
_____
_____
_____
_____
_____
_____
_____
_____
_____
_____
_____
_____
_____
_____
_____
_____
_____

Have you ever had a soulful connection with someone? What did that feel like?

Can you relate to Patricia's experience of a childhood bruise? How so? How do you see this childhood bruise today?

_____
_____
_____
_____
_____
_____
_____
_____
_____
_____
_____
_____
_____
_____
_____
_____
_____
_____
_____
_____
_____
_____
_____

Which story from Cluttered Souls touched you the most? How does this story relate to your life?

_____
_____
_____
_____
_____
_____
_____
_____
_____
_____
_____
_____
_____
_____
_____
_____
_____
_____
_____
_____
_____
_____
_____

Is there something you are fearful of right now? What "untruth" have you been telling yourself?

_____
_____
_____
_____
_____
_____
_____
_____
_____
_____
_____
_____
_____
_____
_____
_____
_____
_____
_____
_____
_____
_____

Imagine what your life would look like fully recovered. How would this change your life?

Personal Notes

About the Author

Patricia Diesel is a life recovery coach and professional organizer dedicated to bringing her skill, inspiration, and encouragement to those who want to regain hope and enhance the quality of their life. She conveys her life-transforming lessons through her travels, speaking engagements, and media appearances, including GMA, Lifetime, and TLC. She has helped countless individuals restore tranquility and a sense of order to their lives.

Patricia is a graduate of the Institute for Professional Excellence in Coaching and the Institute for Challenging Disorganization. She is also a past member of the National Association of Professional Organizers and the National Speakers Association.

Born and raised in New Jersey, Patricia now splits her time between the East Coast and Southern Florida. She has one daughter. You can learn more about Patricia through her website: www.keepitsimplenow.com.

Services, Seminars, and Public Speaking

To inquire about services or to have the author speak to your group or organization, you can write or call directly:

Info@keepitsimplenow.com

(908) 642-1226

For specific questions for the author, write to:

PatriciaDiesel@keepitsimplenow.com

www.ingramcontent.com/pod-product-compliance
Lightning Source LLC
Chambersburg PA
CBHW071150090426
42736CB00012B/2293